Cookies

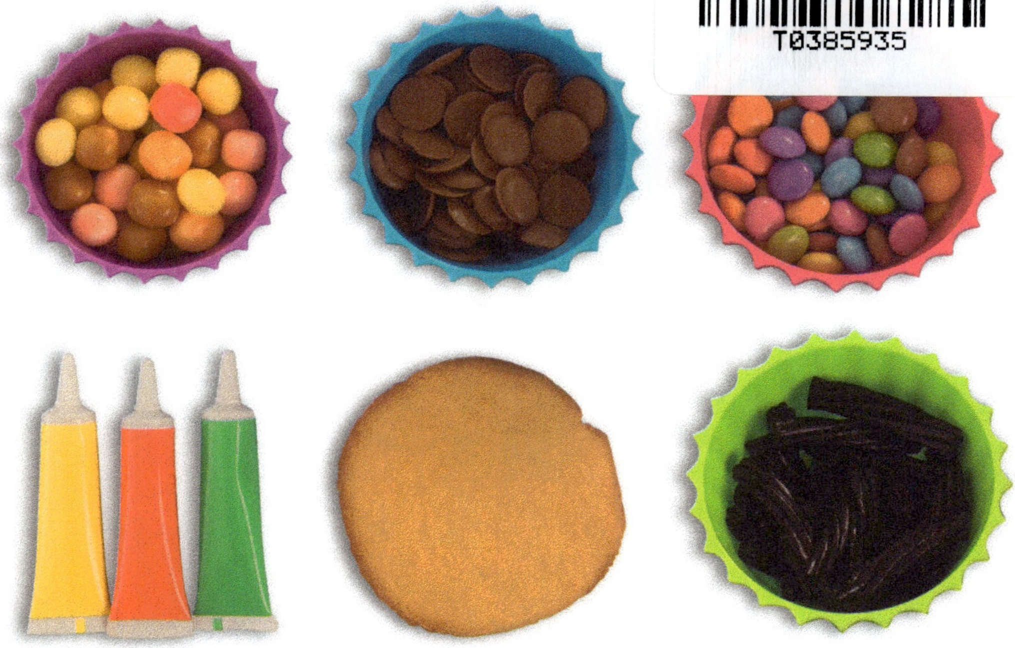

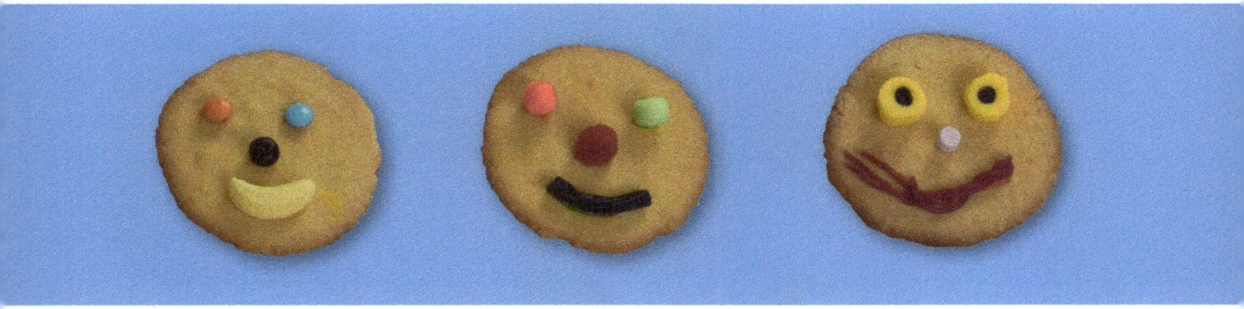

Written by Marie Layson-Dale
Illustrated by Beatrice Costamagna

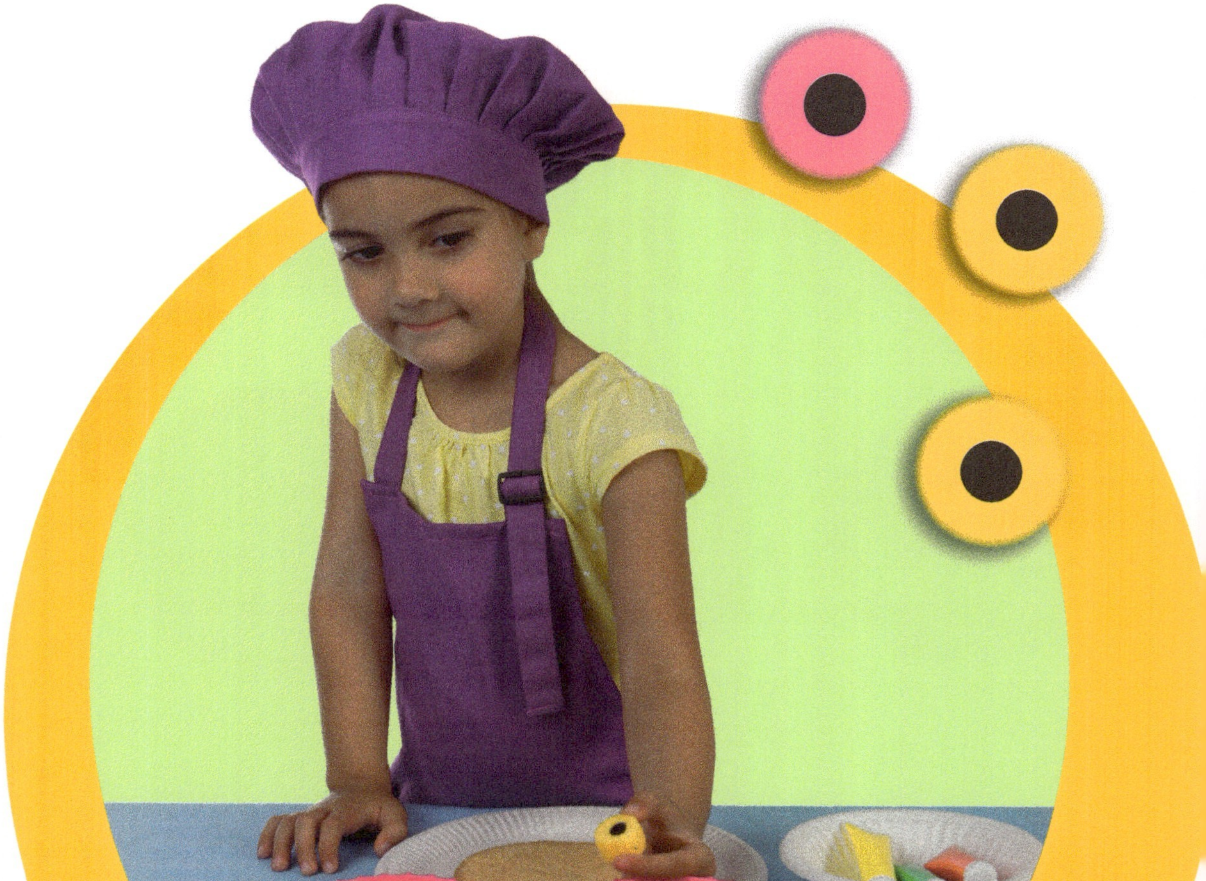

Pick the eyes.

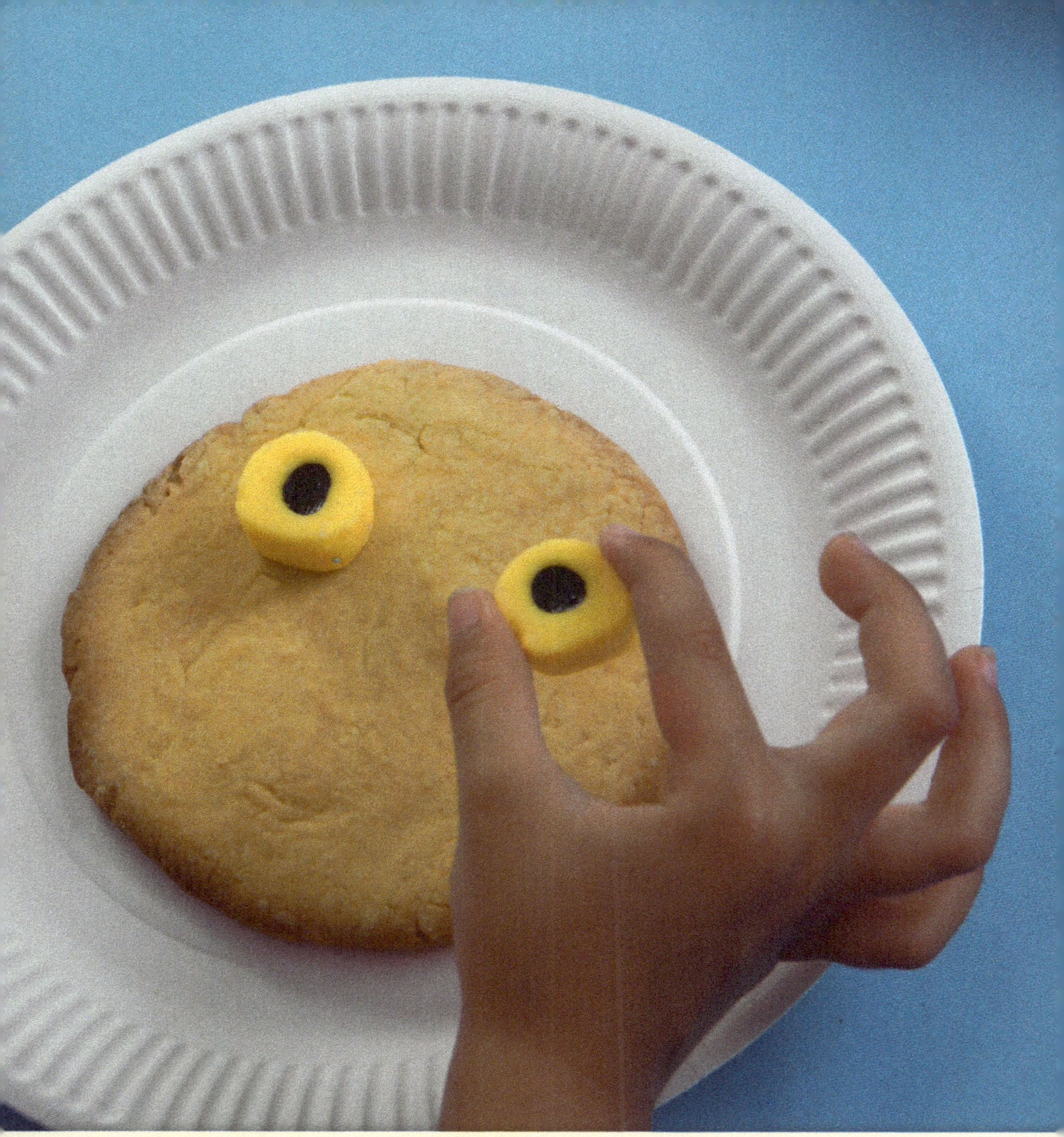

Pop the eyes on.

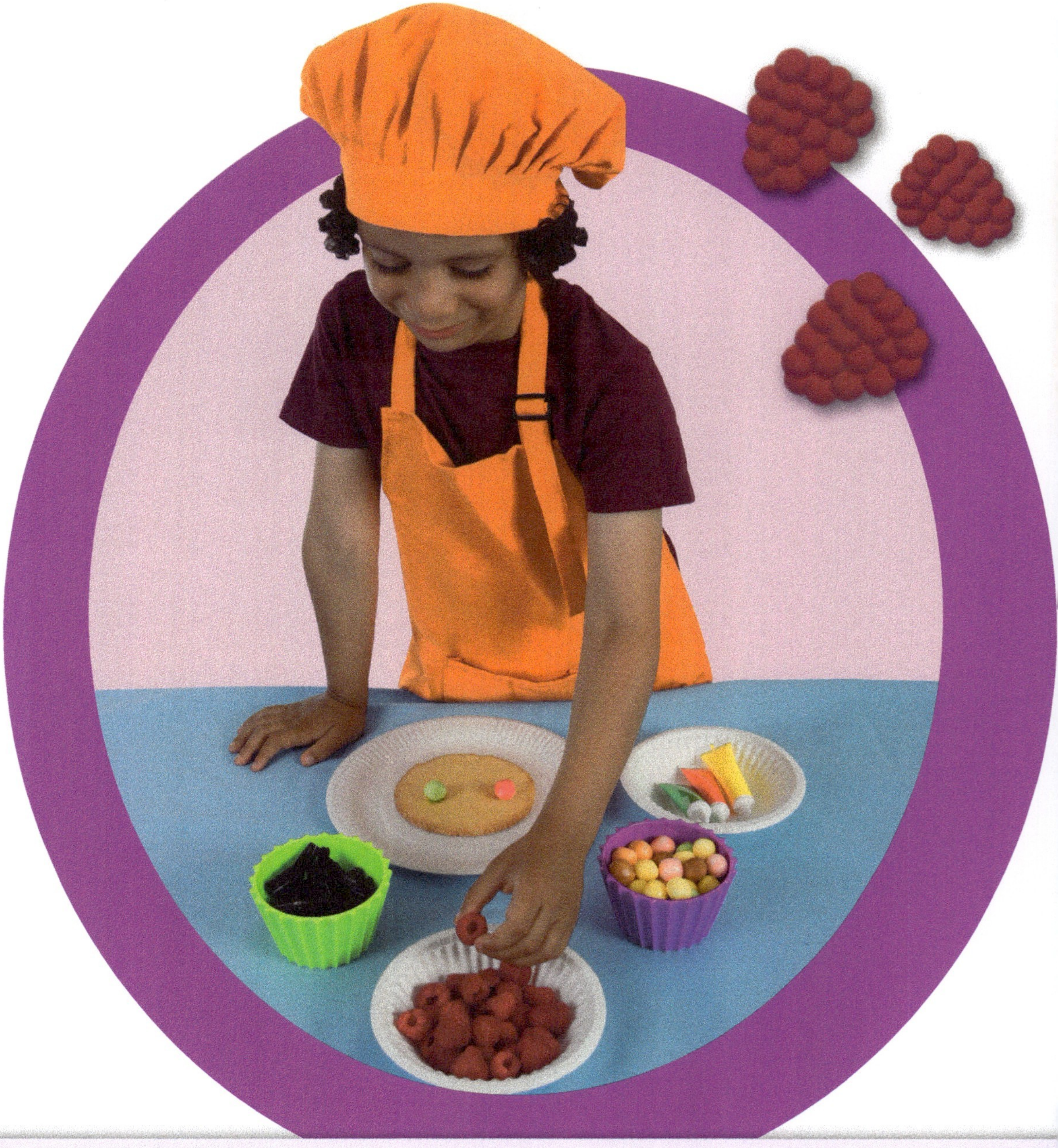

Pick the nose.

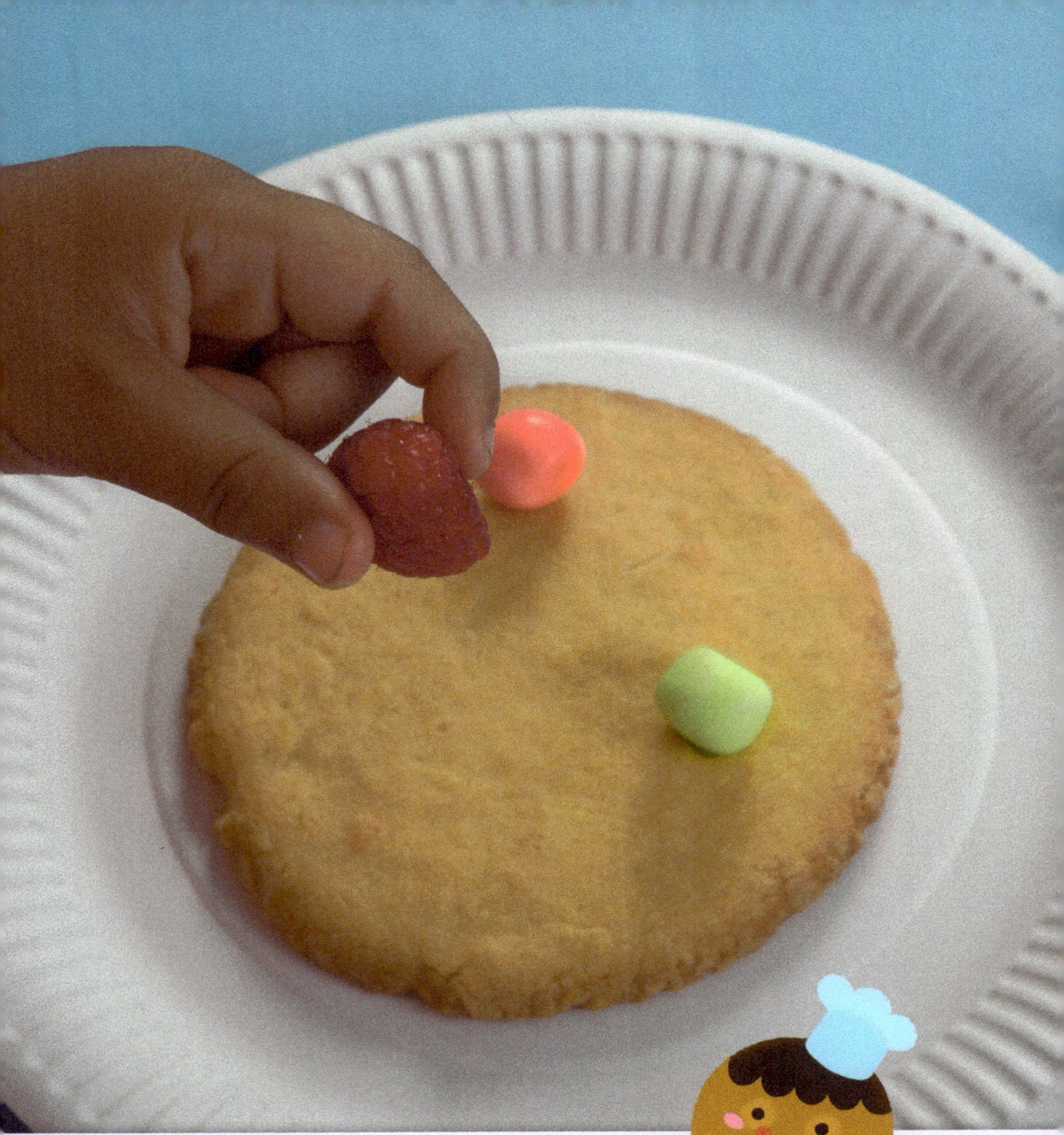

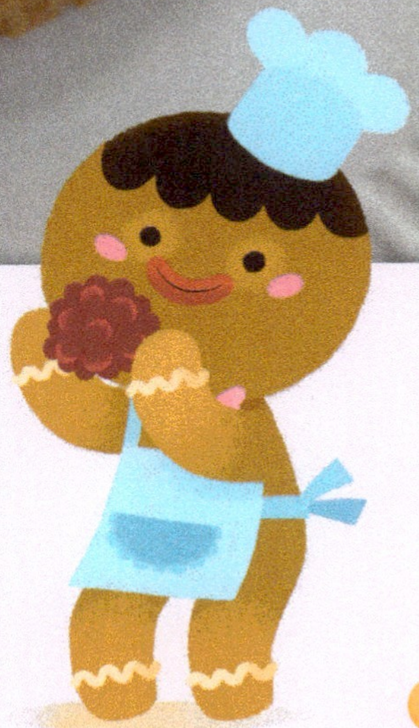

Pop the nose on.

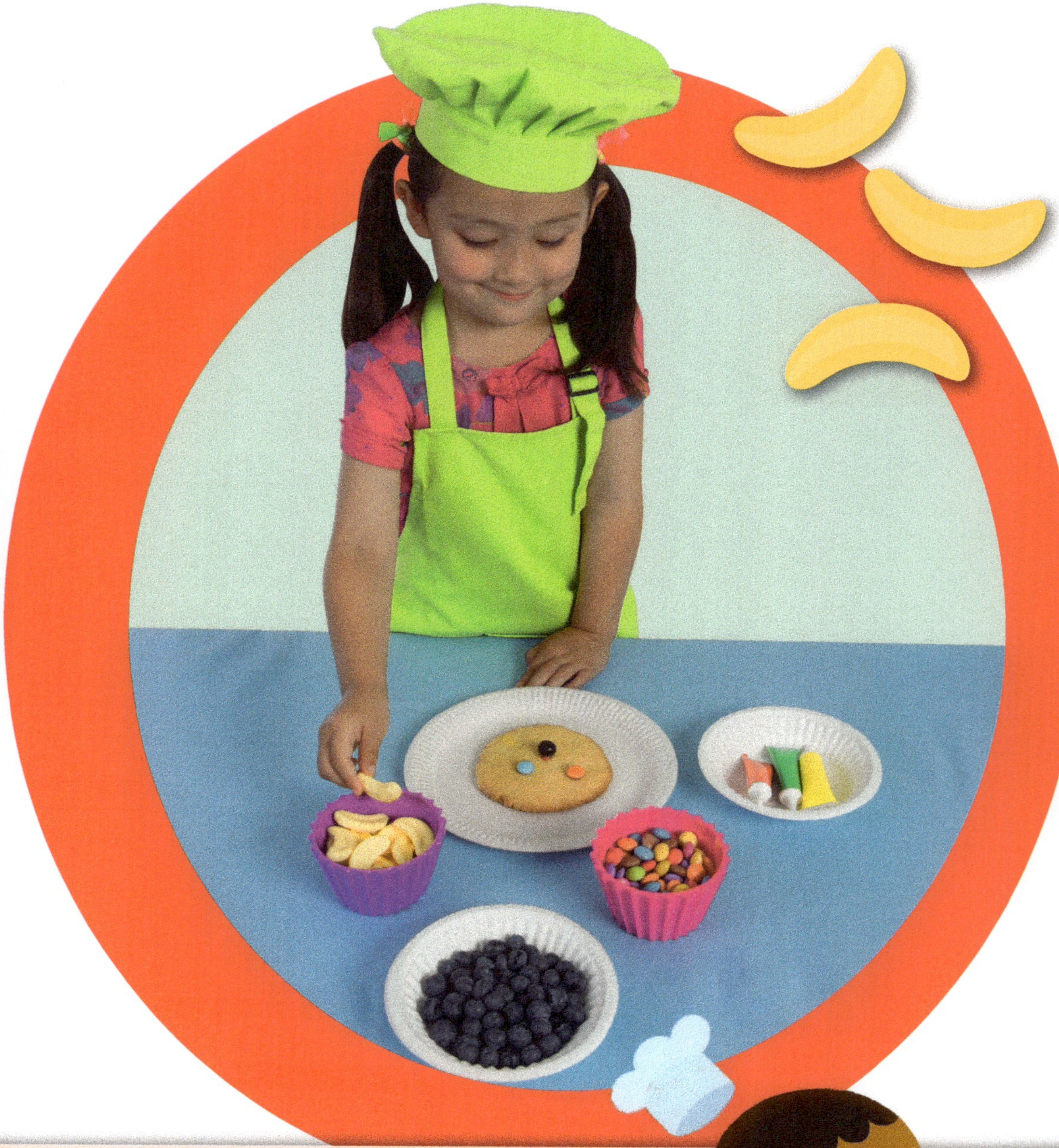

Pick the mouth.

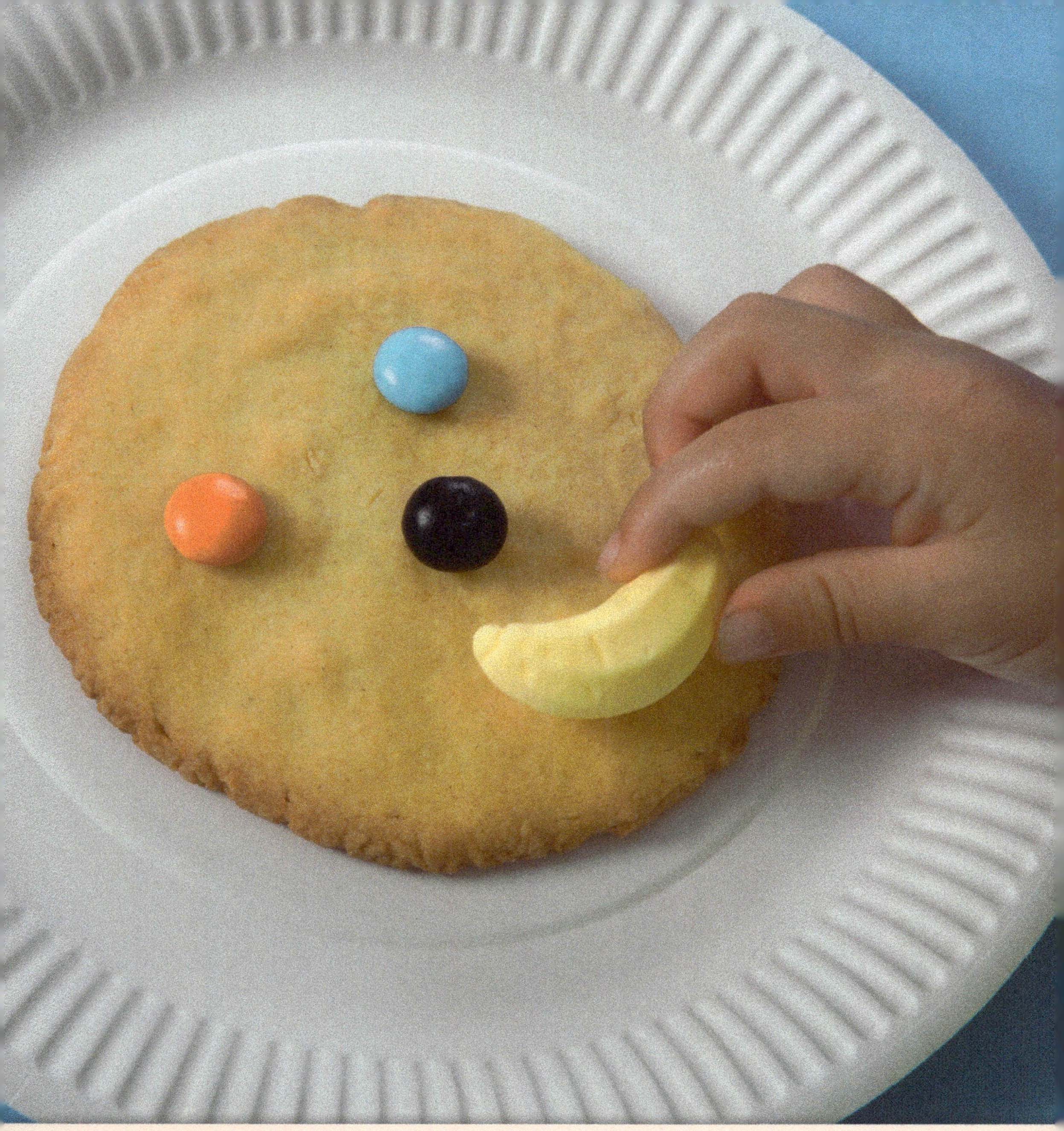

Pop the mouth on.

Pick the cookie!

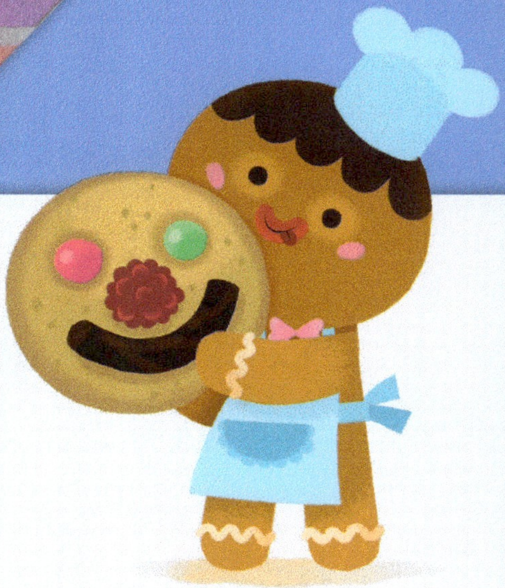